PLAN B

A Gift For:

_____

From:

_____

Published by Hallmark Gift Books,
a division of Hallmark Cards, Inc.,
Kansas City, MO 64141
Visit us on the Web at Hallmark.com.

Editorial Director: Carrie Bolin
Editor: Emily Osborn
Art Director: Chris Opheim
Designer: Rob Latimer
Production Artist: Bryan Ring
Editorial development by Scott Degelman & Associates.

ISBN: 978-1-59530-654-8
BOK1301

Printed and bound in China

God

always

has a

PLAN B

for women

BY OLIVIA SCOTT

Hallmark

INTRODUCTION

God possesses some amazing powers: parting seas, magically providing food from heaven, and even raising the dead.

But one of our Creator's more underrated powers is His ability to turn stumbling blocks into stepping-stones. That's what *God Always Has a Plan B for Women* is all about. One door of opportunity closes, but God opens another one. A failure mysteriously evolves into the key for later success. Bitter rejection becomes the fuel for a new level of focus and determination. As the Bible says, "In all things God works for the good of those who love him" (Romans 8:28).

As you will read in this book, the above verse does not mean that *everything* that happens to us is good. It does mean, however, that God can take the ugly things life hurls at us and somehow make them beautiful. He can bring us through the worst of times and make us stronger, more hopeful, and more grateful women in the process.

Whatever your life challenges might be, our prayer is that this book will help you discover a loving God's Plan B just for you.

Bless you, and thank you for reading.

Olivia Scott

God Always Has a **Plan B**

for Honoring Humble but Heartfelt Beginnings

"Get out there and give real help!
Get out there and love!
Get out there and create
whatever you can to inspire people."

Mother Teresa

Tragedy can bring out the worst in humanity, but it can also bring out the best. When God moves hearts in times of need, amazing things happen.

In May of 2010, Nashville, Tennessee, was hit with devastating floods. A young woman named Susannah Parrish wanted to help. But what could she do? She was a graphic designer, not a trained paramedic, rescue worker, or experienced fund-raiser.

As she thought about the disaster in her community, Susannah felt inspired to design a T-shirt, something she could sell to raise money toward relief efforts. She guessed she might sell a few shirts to friends and to friends of friends. But her design sparked something. Within days, it caught the attention of more than 25,000 people on Facebook. Susannah never dreamed her small effort would make such a difference, but her Nashville Flood Tees—which she sold via a Web site—went on to sell more than 20,000 shirts, enabling her to donate hundreds of thousands of dollars to various relief organizations in the Nashville area.

Susannah says: "People should realize that we are family; we are parts of a body, and each part is needed. Sometimes, when one part of the body is weak, fatigued, or injured, the other parts have to kick in to help out."

Susannah saw herself as one small, humble part of the body, but her unique artistic skill resulted in a much greater result than she could have imagined.

Once her design hit Facebook, thousands of people—of differing ages, races, and religious backgrounds—acted like the body's nerve endings, passing on the message from one cell to another. Charity went viral.

Our varied skills make us effective. Our differences make us rich— rich in the way that truly matters. When we use our special skills to help our fellow human beings, the Giver of those skills can help us accomplish much more than we could ever imagine.

Whatever you give is acceptable
if you give it eagerly.
And give according to what you have,
not what you don't have.

2 Corinthians 8:12 (NLT)

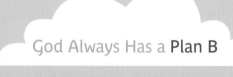

God Always Has a **Plan B**

for Making You an Encourager

_"You never know when a moment
and a few sincere words
can have an impact on a life."_

Zig Ziglar

"Here's how to identify someone who needs encouragement," goes the old saying. "That person is breathing."

Especially in today's age of cynicism and instant Internet criticism, encouragement matters more than ever. It helps take away the sting of that cruel comment one might hear at work, at home, or via social media. Sometimes, encouragement renews hopes and dreams. It can even change a life. Encouragement is a critical need of every person, family, school, community, and workplace.

Everyone needs encouragement, and everyone who receives encouragement is changed by it. To encourage people is to help them gain courage they might not otherwise find—courage to face the day, to do what's right, to make a difference. Many of us women are naturally good encouragers, but this is a gift that anyone can share. At its heart, encouragement is all about communicating a person's value. When people feel valuable, they feel capable, and, most of all, loved.

As you seek to encourage your husband, children, co-workers, friends, or whomever, look for opportunities like the ones below:

When people are struggling to do the right thing, stand with them.

When people are striving to face a big challenge, empower them.

When people are working toward a goal, motivate them.

When people are looking for a place to belong, welcome them.

When people are seeking some recognition or validation, honor them.

Indeed, encouragement can take many forms. If you are stuck for ideas, think about what inspires and encourages *you*. A handwritten note or card? A surprise phone call? A clever text or e-mail message? An invitation to lunch or coffee? A personalized gift basket? Gestures like these can do so much to bless others—and you as well. It just takes a bit of time and effort.

Today, why not give someone (and yourself) the gift of encouragement?

Pleasant words are as an honeycomb,
sweet to the soul,
and health to the bones.

Proverbs 16:24 (KJV)

for Bringing Light to Dark Places

*"One great, strong, unselfish soul in every community
could actually redeem the world."*

Elbert Hubbard

Jeannine Brabon is one of the last people you'd expect to find in the jaws of hell. But that's where she spends much of her time.

Jeannine, a native Colombian, is a serious academic, a professor at Seminario Biblico de Colombia (the Biblical Seminary of Colombia). She is a Hebrew scholar, specializing in biblical Hebrew and its interpretation. Among her many accomplishments is translating the massive LaSor's *Handbook of Biblical Hebrew* into Spanish.

But Jeannine is also a missionary, and this calling flows from her work in the classroom. "I teach people who have had their fathers, brothers, and sons assassinated," she explains. "I rarely have a class in any given year in which a student doesn't lose a family member to a violent death. Life is of little value. It's a deadly and dangerous world. But security is not the absence of danger, it's the presence of Jesus."

One day, a girl named Margarita (one of Jeannine's students) asked for help searching for her brother, who had been missing for five days. Their search led them to the city morgue of Medellin (pronounced "med-duh jean"), home to the infamous drug cartel. Medellin sees an average of twenty-five criminally related deaths every day, with more than a hundred in a typical weekend.

At the morgue, the teacher and student encountered more than a hundred bodies on their search.

Jeannine says she will never forget Margarita's cries when she found her brother, who had been brutally tortured to death. As Jeannine and her student cried together, a question exploded in the professor's mind: "What can I do? What *can* I do?"

Shortly after that experience, Jeannine was invited to speak at Medellin's Bellavista Prison, which has earned the nickname "Jaws of Hell." In the mid-1970s, the prison was built to house 1,500 inmates. In the years that followed, Bellavista's population swelled to more than 6,600 dangerous criminals: drug lords, terrorists, assassins for hire.

At Bellavista's worst point, dead bodies, some of them decapitated, littered the prison floor. Walls were covered with graffiti, written in blood.

Prison riots were commonplace, and Bellavista averaged forty-five murders a month. Often, the guards were so terrified that they refused to pass through the prison gates to report for work. The prison had become, essentially, a training ground for Medellin's killing fields. Once outside the prison walls, either through parole or escape, a Bellavista ex-con would likely join the ranks of the city's 3,000 contract criminals—criminals who specialize in blackmail, kidnapping, and murder. Or, one could join any of the more than 120 gangs, all ready to kill for pay. According to one Colombian newspaper, the country was averaging 25,000 murders annually. And Medellin was a major source of the country's woes.

So, not surprisingly, the invitation from Bellavista left an unassuming female missionary-professor feeling inadequate. And terrified. But Jeannine clung to this verse: "The wicked flee when no man pursueth: but the righteous are bold as a lion" (Proverbs 28:1, KJV).

Standing in front of her criminal audience, Jeannine preached about

God's steadfast love. As she concluded, twenty-three crying men came forward to dedicate their lives to Jesus.

That was only the beginning.

Jeannine soon launched a Bible training school, the Bible Training Institute, within Bellavista's walls. She spends two days a week inside the prison, teaching inmates about Jesus' life-transforming love. The institute's rigorous two-year curriculum transforms inmates into spiritual leaders. The program is no joke. When an inmate graduates, the dean of Seminario Biblico de Colombia hands him a diploma.

More than forty inmates study at the institute at a given time, and the total number of graduates has topped one thousand.

Jeannine Brabon does more than teach in the Jaws of Hell. She meets with law enforcement officers, politicians, and prison officials to advocate for better conditions, such as basic sanitation for the prisoners. She witnesses to prisoners and guards.

Not surprisingly, some in Medellin don't appreciate hit men, drug lords, and terrorists "going soft" and losing their value to the drug cartel. Thus, Jeannine lives under the constant threat of death. Her movements are tracked by Medellin's criminal element, forcing her to regularly change her daily routines and travel routes.

Once, an inmate infiltrated one of Jeannine's prayer groups and later made a false accusation about her to a powerful guerilla commander. The commander issued a death decree.

When the inmate heard about the decree, however, he panicked. Guilt-stricken, he rushed to Jeannine and confessed what he had done. Then he informed the guerilla commander that he had levied false charges. The death threat was lifted.

Jeannine was matter-of-fact about her brush with death. "We are not to fear those who kill the body," she said. "We are to fear the sin that will destroy us eternally. Our greatest concern ought to be that we die to sin daily."

Meanwhile, despite the cloud of danger that is Jeannine's constant companion, Bellavista Prison continues to experience what can only be called a revival. At one crucial point in the prison's history, its riots threatened to spill over into the city. It appeared that the military would have to be called in. The media gathered, expecting to cover a massacre. However, instead of unleashing the Colombian army, the prison warden honored the request of a small group of Christian townspeople. Inspired by Jeannine, they wanted to hold a prayer meeting—inside the prison walls.

While the riots raged, the small band of believers prayed fervently. Soon, prisoners began turning in their weapons—not to the guards but to a former inmate who was now a volunteer chaplain. This chaplain had earned the prisoners' trust, reporting to his post at 8 o'clock every morning for three years and ministering within Bellavista's walls—regardless of how bad prison conditions were on any given day. He showed up when the guards would not.

Jeannine described the disaster averted in clear terms: "God is moving in unprecedented ways. The Holy Spirit is giving life where death reigns."

Today, those who have seen it describe Bellavista as "a model prison"—a most unlikely beacon of hope in a land darkened by evil. More than 150 faithful inmates pack the prison chapel for daily services at dawn. Smaller groups meet twice daily on prison patios and pavilions. A daily radio broadcast offers counseling and helps inmates communicate their newfound faith to their families. During weekend visitations, inmates hold evangelistic services for their family and friends.

In a recent thirteen-year period, Bellavista saw zero riots and the murder rate dropped to less than one per year, a fraction of the forty-five monthly killings the prison once endured.

One telling sign of Bellavista's transformation occurred after the terrorist attacks of September 11, 2001. The Colombian prisoners committed themselves to praying for the United States and all those affected by the tragedy. As a show of their ongoing prayer and support, a few prisoners carved a sculpture of praying hands, which was eventually delivered to then-President George W. Bush. The president kept the carving in the Oval Office to remind him of the faithful prayers of a group of former drug lords, terrorists, and hit men.

How was one woman able to start a movement of peace and spiritual revival in the Jaws of Hell? Perhaps it is fitting to give one of Bellavista's inmates the last word:

"God chose what is foolish in the world to shame the wise," says the convict. "God chose what is weak in the world to shame the strong. God chose what is low and despised in the world so that no human being might boast in the presence of God."

(Author's Note: This story is based on information from the Web sites of Prison Fellowship and Urbana Ministries as well as from firsthand accounts of visitors to Bellavista Prison.)

I'll call nobodies and make them somebodies;
I'll call the unloved and make them beloved.
In the place where they yelled out,
"You're nobody!" they're calling you
"God's living children."

Romans 9:25-26 (MSG)

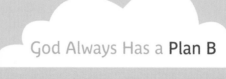

God Always Has a **Plan B**

for Rewarding Faithful Effort

*"It takes a lot of courage
to show your dreams to someone else."*

Erma Bombeck

Have you ever heard one of your girlfriends, relatives, or even your sweetheart say something like this: "I could have done something really great in life; I just never got that big break."

The sad thing is that so many people *could* have accomplished something great if they had seized all of their little opportunities and breaks—instead of waiting for the Big One.

God blesses us when we live gratefully and purposefully, whatever our circumstances. He blesses us when we grab opportunity, even when it doesn't come in our preferred size and shape.

Consider this example: A young woman dreamed of writing for the masses, but that dream seemed a world away from her actual job as a lowly copy editor for a small-town newspaper. She felt fortunate to have *any* job in publishing. After all, one of her college instructors had told her, "Forget about being a writer."

Nonetheless, she graduated with an English degree and found a paper that would pay her (modestly) for her writing skills. But those skills were confined to the obituaries, considered one of the lowest rungs on the newspaper ladder.

Meanwhile, the woman married, and she and her husband tried to conceive without success. Their family doctor told them they would never be able to have a baby. So they adopted a daughter. Less than a year later, the woman got pregnant. In fact, she got pregnant four times during the next four years. Sadly, only two of those babies survived childbirth.

For the next twenty years, this writer, wife, and mother toiled at low-level newspaper jobs. Finally, she convinced one of her editors to let her write a weekly humor column . . . for $3 per piece. A year later, the editor sweetened the pot. Somewhat. He bumped the column's frequency to three times a week. And he told her he would try to syndicate the column to other papers.

More than 900 newspapers responded favorably.

For the next thirty years, Erma Bombeck wrote her column, which was eagerly read by more than thirty million people in the United States and Canada. Best-selling books followed. Her face graced the cover of *Time* and other national publications. She was awarded a host of honorary degrees. She was, arguably, America's best-known humor writer.

Erma wrote with wit and charm, despite trials in her personal life. She endured breast cancer and kidney failure. On the professional front, she wrote a sitcom that was canned after just a few episodes. She penned a Broadway play that never opened.

During the last few years of her life, she faced daily dialysis. But she kept on writing. She made America laugh and sometimes cry. When she passed away at age sixty-nine, it was national news. America knew it had lost one of its most entertaining and gracious voices.

Looking back at her life's ups and downs, Bombeck noted, "I am not a failure. I did fail at some things. But it's a big difference between the two."

Erma Bombeck's life is a lesson to us all. Our failings do not make us failures. Sometimes, a failure is just the beginning of a great life story. Don't let setbacks derail your dreams.

I will wait on the LORD . . .
And I will hope in Him.
Here am I.

Isaiah 8:17-18 (NKJV)

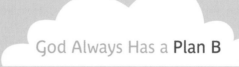

God Always Has a **Plan B**

for Turning Endings Into Beginnings

"I have held many things in my hands,
and I have lost them all;
but whatever I have placed in God's hands,
that I still possess."

Martin Luther

Andrea Jaeger was not your typical middle-schooler. While many of her classmates were experiencing their first romantic crushes, the fourteen-year-old Chicago native was crushing the world's best tennis players. Displaying athleticism and a preternaturally powerful forehand, she defeated legends like Chris Evert, Martina Navratilova, Tracy Austin, and Billie Jean King. Not long after blowing out the candles on her fifteenth birthday cake, she became the youngest player ever to be seeded at Wimbledon. By the time she was sixteen, she was the second-ranked tennis player in the world.

Andrea's outsized ability—combined with her endearing braces and blond pigtails—made her a media darling. But away from the tennis spotlight, Andrea's life, in her parlance, "sucked." Her high school classmates resented her success, which isolated her from most of her peers. In the lunchroom, students tossed food at her. In the hallways, they threw her into lockers. "It wasn't a fun time to grow up," she understates.

But the abuse didn't harden Andrea's heart; it made her more compassionate. At age fifteen, she was riding in a limo, returning to her hotel after a tennis match in New Jersey. When the car approached a toy store, she asked the driver to stop. She dashed into the store and bought several hundred dollars' worth of toys, which she then delivered to children in the critical-care unit of New York's Helen Hayes Hospital. "I just felt a calling at that moment," she would explain later.

As her life on the pro tennis circuit continued, Andrea continued to surprise hospitalized kids with visits and gifts purchased with her prize money. The compassion she held for children hummed inside her, like a hunger that would never be sated.

But at only nineteen, with years of her best tennis ahead of her, Andrea Jaeger was aced by misfortune. She suffered a shoulder injury that would soon end her career.

She spent no time crying into her pigtails, however. She accepted that she could no longer be a tennis champion, and she committed her life to being a champion of children in need. She threw herself into creating a foundation for children with cancer. The one-time world-class athlete took a job as an airline ticket agent so that she could use the air miles she accrued to conduct research, raise funds, and visit sick children.

Andrea spent years building infrastructure for her foundation. Several tennis players contributed to the cause. A married couple donated ten acres of land. A businessman provided $1.7 million to build an 18,000-square-foot facility. For her part, Andrea poured her tennis earnings, about $1.4 million, into the effort.

Finally, at age twenty-five, she launched The Silver Lining Foundation in Aspen, Colorado. The Silver Lining's mission is simple: To make life better for terminally ill kids. Every year, The Silver Lining welcomes children from across the country. They receive counseling and emotional support. They get to escape the daunting challenges in their lives and lose themselves in the pure abandon of activities like horseback riding and whitewater rafting.

As one of the foundation's volunteers describes it, Andrea Jaeger helps children "abandon being treated like a sick person. The children really bloom."

"Andrea does this for all the right reasons," says model-actress Cindy Crawford, a frequent The Silver Lining volunteer. "It shines through her actions. She is utterly selfless and completely devoted to helping others."

Today, Andrea divides her time between working directly with kids in Colorado and traveling the country to raise money toward her foundation's $2 million annual budget. She also underwrites reunions and retreats for families affected by cancer, provides college scholarships, and brings The Silver Lining programs to the doorsteps of children who are too sick to travel.

Additionally, she has launched two other humanitarian efforts. The Little Star Foundation expands on the mission of The Silver Lining, assisting children affected by disease, neglect, and poverty. The Little Star's first major benefactor was John McEnroe, known as tennis's notorious, tantrum-throwing "bad boy" during his playing days.

The other effort, Athletes for Hope, encourages sports stars to be more charitable people, to use their resources and influence for the good of humanity, especially the needy. Among those who have joined Jaeger in this cause are Andre Agassi, Lance Armstrong, Tony Hawk, and Muhammad Ali.

Those who interact with the former tennis star these days refer to her as Sister Andrea. In 2006, she gave up all her material possessions and was ordained by the Episcopal Church as an Anglican Dominican nun.

A journey from teen tennis phenom to philanthropist-nun might seem bizarre, but Sister Andrea doesn't see it that way. "By giving me such a talent for the sport of tennis," she explains, "God gave me the chance to prepare for bigger challenges and purposes in my life."

Looking back on the career-ending injury at age nineteen, Sister Andrea is similarly philosophical. Even as a teen, she explains, she had her eyes and heart set on something more significant than tennis. "My family and friends were so upset when I got hurt," she recalls, "but I knew in my heart that I was called to help kids. Because of how I was treated when I was younger, I know this: everyone can use someone who cares."

Words we all would do well to take to heart.

*Make a careful exploration of who you are
and the work you have been given,
and then sink yourself into that.
Don't be impressed with yourself.
Don't compare yourself with others.
Each of you must take responsibility
for doing the creative best you can
with your own life.*

Galatians 6:4–5 (MSG)

God Always Has a **Plan B**

for Making the Ordinary Extraordinary

*"All the beautiful sentiments in the world
weigh less than a single lovely action."*

James Russell Lowell

Has this ever happened to you?

You've folded that last T-shirt, paid that last bill, or answered that last e-mail. But then, instead of mentally checking another task off your to-do list or shaking your head at the monotony of daily life, you smile. You lean back and breathe deeply. You feel satisfied, centered. True, you haven't cured any disease or solved world hunger, but you've done something well. You have made your home (your life!) more organized and more efficient. *Better*. And for this, it's good to thank God.

You see, in the common tasks of every day we can find ourselves at our most focused, disciplined, and poised. We work with no ulterior motives. This is all about keeping one's life moving forward, not veering off into the weeds. This is about bringing skill and dedication and, yes, love to the mundane. In the process, we transform the mundane into the meaningful.

Do you *love* every one of your daily tasks? Probably not. But can you do every task with love—love for a husband, a child, and life itself? Yes. Can you do it with love for the God who makes it all possible? Yes. Most definitely, yes.

When we are present in the everyday moments, we find that God is present with us. And where God is, the flicker of a holy flame can help us see the commonplace in a whole new light.

Where your treasure is,
there your heart will be also.

Matthew 6:21 (NKJV)

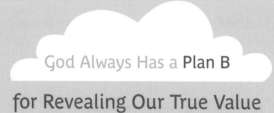

God Always Has a **Plan B**

for Revealing Our True Value

"Purpose is what gives a life meaning."

Charles H. Parkhurst

Every now and then, a new TV commercial appears, trumpeting the virtues of the latest technology in nonstick cookware. Who knew that a simple frying pan could be "revolutionary"? According to the ads, some of today's pots and pans are so advanced, it seems one could cook glue in them and even *that* wouldn't stick.

Some people are like "miracle pans." Nothing seems to stick to them. No sadness. No insult. No mistake. They seem impervious to everything.

Most of us, however, find that *everything* sticks. We try to get rid of that annoying crud, but it won't be scrubbed away, even with vigorous effort and industrial-strength cleansers.

That is where God comes in. We don't have to be spotless for Him. We don't have to pretend, "There's nothing wrong here! There's nothing bad stuck to me!"

God meets us where we are. We don't have to get to a certain point on our spiritual path before He will show up.

Yes, He meets us *where* we are and *as* we are. With all the dried-on sin and shame and insecurity. With all the scrapes and scratches, dings and dents.

Perhaps the apostle Paul said it best: "We have this treasure in jars of clay" (2 Corinthians 4:7). Let's never miss the importance of this imagery. Paul said jars of *clay*, not pure gold. Not space-age alloys. Let's face it: we are not the most amazing containers on the market. But inside we hold treasure.

May the brilliance and power of the treasure we hold inside us give us purpose and love. No matter what might be sticking to us on the outside.

> If you only look at us, you might well miss the brightness.
> We carry this precious Message around
> in the unadorned clay pots of our ordinary lives.
>
> 2 Corinthians 4:7 (MSG)

God Always Has a **Plan B**

for Defying the Odds

*"The circumstances of our lives have as much power
as we choose to give them."*

David McNally

Jean Driscoll was born with spina bifida, a congenital birth defect
in which the spinal column fails to close completely. Thus, doctors
painted a bleak picture for Jean's parents: She would never walk. She
wouldn't be able to attend traditional schools. And she would be
dependent on others for the rest of her life.

Jean has spent her life proving those doctors wrong.

At age two, she was fitted with leg braces that allowed her to walk—
although "walk" is a generous term. The young girl staggered from side
to side, dragging her feet and fighting to maintain her balance. But she
was moving, by her own power and determination.

As she grew older, Jean insisted on being included in neighborhood
games, including footraces. She excelled at crawling through obstacle
courses, and she became adept at the basketball marksmanship game
H-O-R-S-E. She developed a right-handed set shot, using her left hand
to grab a fence, mailbox, or other prop for stability.

In the fourth grade, despite protests from her parents, Jean taught
herself to ride a bike. Exhilarated by the achievement, she spent one
Saturday cruising up and down a sidewalk for eight straight hours.

Eventually, she graduated from a kid's bike with training wheels to a ten-speed. But as a young teen, she ended up crashing that ten-speed and dislocating her left hip. She endured five operations and a year living in a body cast as she recovered. When the cast was finally removed, the hip promptly dislocated again.

Because of the accident—and her weak lower-body muscles—doctors said Jean would need crutches and a wheelchair to get around. And when she returned to school at age fifteen, classmates made fun of her because of the wheelchair.

Jean Driscoll was devastated. Privately, she contemplated suicide. "I couldn't make myself comfortable with the chair," she recalls. "I would ask God, 'Why don't you pick on somebody else?'"

She tried to find herself academically, but after completing high school, she flunked out of college after three semesters.

On the social front, she didn't seek out boyfriends like her sisters did, afraid the chair would be an impossible barrier to romance and commitment. "I thought my life was over," she says flatly.

In reality, however, life was just beginning. And the hated wheelchair was the thing that got her rolling in the right direction.

After flunking out of college, Jean took a job as a live-in nanny for a young family. During this time, she met Brad Hedrick, a coach at the University of Illinois. Hedrick spoke at a wheelchair sports clinic and watched Jean and some others try their hand at a game of wheelchair soccer.

Jean Driscoll caught the coach's eye. "I saw lots of enthusiasm and talent," he says. "Unchanneled at the time."

While Jean's skill was unpolished, Hedrick was impressed by her speed. Soon, he recruited her to play wheelchair basketball at the University of Illinois, home to the nation's top collegiate program. He didn't have to recruit very hard. His new prospect felt like she had found something that had been missing her whole life: Something that came naturally to her. Something she could do really well.

Jean went on to letter all four years for the Illini and was a three-time MVP. In her junior and senior years, she led her team to the national championship. As a senior, she was named Women's Sports Foundation

Amateur Athlete of the Year.

Beyond the athletic achievements, the one-time dropout graduated with distinction, earning a bachelor's degree in speech communication. Then, she went on to earn a master's in rehabilitation administration.

But even with all these accomplishments, Jean Driscoll wasn't done defying odds.

With her basketball career behind her, she turned her attention to wheelchair races. Her competitive athletic nature took over from there. She set out with a simple goal: to become the world's best wheelchair racer.

A businessman donated a racing wheelchair for her to use in her first national race, the Phoenix Sun-Times 10K. With almost no training, she placed a respectable third in the 6.2-mile race. So she intensified her training. Soon, she was winning a variety of races, nationally and internationally. At her first major international competition, in England, she won nine gold medals. Her new coach, Marty Morse, encouraged her to try the marathon. She spent two years preparing to handle the longer distance, and in her first try at 26.2 miles, she finished the 1989 Chicago Marathon in under two hours (which is faster than the world-record for runners).

Her Chicago performance qualified her for the prestigious Boston Marathon. In Beantown in 1990, she rolled her way to a world record. And she was just getting started. The 1990 Boston debut was just the first of eight Boston Marathon victories. Her quickest Boston time, 1 hour, 34 minutes, and 22 seconds, still stands as the world record.

Jean was relentless in her pursuit to become the world's No. 1 wheelchair racer. She logged as many as 130 miles every week. Her commitment to her training regimen earned her the nickname "Jean Machine" around her hometown of Champaign, Illinois. Sometimes, she would invite as many as five people to latch onto her wheelchair and offer resistance as she powered up a steep hill.

And when she wasn't rolling at high speed on the roads or the track, she was in the weight room pumping iron. Though only 5 feet tall and 110 pounds, she could bench-press 200 pounds. "I love being in shape," the formerly depressed teen proclaimed. "I love being fit and strong."

"Fit and strong" is something of an understatement. Jean reached a fitness level that allowed her to power her wheelchair at almost 17 miles an hour—well under a 4-minute-per-mile pace—for 20-plus miles. And even that brisk average speed is deceiving. On downhill portions of races like Boston, she reached top speeds of 50 miles an hour and 130 wheel revolutions per minute.

The Jean Machine's early success in road races caught the attention of the US Olympic team. She competed at the Olympic Games in 1992 and 1996 (where wheelchair races were exhibition events). Additionally, she made four US Paralympic teams. (The Paralympic Games, a sister event to the traditional Olympic Games, is held every four years, in the same city as the Olympic Games.) Jean competed in a variety of distances at the 1988, 1992, 1996, and 2000 Paralympics, earning at least one gold medal at each.

In the process, she found that she was rolling right through the boundaries that once confined her. "I'm not a disabled person," she declared. "I'm an elite athlete who's training for the same reasons as any other world-class athlete. I want to be the best in the world in my sport. I want to make a difference."

Jean Driscoll retired from elite competition late in the year 2000, after a stellar thirteen-year career. In addition to the marathon world record, she also holds the world-best mark in the 10,000-meter track race, set at the 1996 Paralympics.

Today, she speaks nationally, encouraging a variety of people to remain hopeful, even in dire circumstances. "God has given me an incredible platform," she says, "and I'm really enjoying using it. For young people and adults, the biggest limitations are the ones you place on yourself. But if you're willing to take risks, dream big, and work hard, you'll meet goals you never thought you could."

We know that God causes everything
to work together for the good of those
who love God and are called according
to his purpose for them.

Romans 8:28 (NLT)

for Asking (and Answering) the Right Questions

"Love multiplies. It does not divide."

Kristin Armstrong

Here are fifteen things God will not ask of any woman (or man):

1. God won't ask what kind of car you drove but how many times you offered rides to those with no transportation.

2. God won't ask the square footage of your house or apartment but how many people you welcomed into it.

3. God won't ask about the fancy clothes you had in your closet but how many of those clothes found their way to the needy.

4. God won't ask about your social status but what kind of *personal* class you displayed.

5. God won't ask how many material possessions you had but whether or not those material things possessed *you*.

6. God won't ask your highest salary but if you compromised your character to achieve it.

7. God won't ask how much overtime you worked but if you worked overtime for your friends and family.

8. God won't ask how many promotions you received but how you promoted others.

9. God won't ask what your job title was but if you performed that job to the best of your ability.

10. God won't ask what you did to help yourself but what you did to help others.

11. God won't ask how many friends you've had but if you were a true friend to those in your life.

12. God won't ask what you did to protect your rights but what you did to protect the rights of others.

13. God won't ask in what neighborhood you lived but how you treated your neighbors.

14. God won't ask about your beauty on the outside but your beauty on the inside.

15. God won't ask about what you *said* you would do but rather about what you actually did.

The lines of purpose in your lives never grow slack,
tightly tied as they are to your future in heaven,
kept taut by hope.

Colossians 1:5 (MSG)

God Always Has a **Plan B**

for Helping You Get Real

A man who thought he had an amazing replica of a Leonardo da Vinci painting took his work of art to a museum. He showed the copied painting to the curator to get her reaction.

To the man's surprise, the curator immediately identified the painting as a fake. Then, she went on to name the copyist, his nationality, and the likely date of the painting's creation.

"But how could you know all that so quickly?" the man sputtered. "I have seen pictures of the da Vinci original, and this likeness seems really, really good to me."

The curator smiled. "People who make a living copying the masters have little imagination of their own," she explained. "This painter's particular choice of subject, brush strokes, and areas of color emphasis practically scream 'Copy!' Think of those celebrity impersonators you see on TV. You know how they overemphasize vocal inflections, catchphrases, and gestures? It's the same thing with people who impersonate painters."

This true story holds an important lesson for today's woman. We are blessed with a wide variety of inspirational role models: businesswomen, athletes, artists, and more. But this blessing can backfire on us. If we want to distinguish ourselves, we need to be innovators, not imitators. It is great to gain inspiration from someone we admire, but we should be inspired to develop our own distinctive styles. The world does not need clones of so-called "successful power women." It needs the one and only YOU!

Do not neglect your gift.

1 Timothy 4:14 (NKJV)

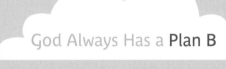

God Always Has a **Plan B**

for Finding Lost Perspective

"When we wake up in the morning
and turn our soul toward You,
You are there first."

Søren Kierkegaard

It's amazing how minor irritations can take a woman's eyes off God. Tension headaches interrupt our sleep. Telemarketers interrupt our dinnertime. Corporate restructurings interrupt our career progress. Workplace "emergencies" interrupt our vacations. And, to be fair, troubles on the home front often interrupt us at work.

When we get a case of "Life, Interrupted," we must step back and try to regain our perspective. Will the world stop turning if we don't quite make that project deadline? Will babies no longer smile and birds no longer sing if we can't do absolutely everything we want while on vacation? Will our job become less meaningful if a less deserving person gets "Associate of the Month"?

When we look at life clearly, what is a traffic ticket or flat tire or flight delay when we compare them to being loved wholly and eternally by Almighty God?

What's more, what can possibly compare to being made clean from all our sins? Even when life is hard, life is still good. Because our God is *good*.

Who of you by being worried can
add a single hour to his life?

Matthew 6:27 (NASB)

God Always Has a **Plan B**

for Putting Proof Into Promises

*"It is not the magnitude of our actions
but the amount of love that is put into them that matters."*

Mother Teresa

Think about the last time you heard a politician make a promise. What was your reaction? An eye roll? A weary sigh? Maybe a sarcastic "Yeah, *right!*"

Yes, at this point in the twenty-first century, promises and oaths are not what they used to be. We've been burned too many times. We've seen that words, no matter how sincerely they are uttered, can be hollow. Your manager or your mayor says, "I promise." You counter, "Prove it."

No wonder God's promises stand out from the crowd. They have substance. It's certainly no accident that so many of God's promises have been accompanied by very tangible (and very memorable) signs and wonders: Moses' burning bush, Aaron's magical rod, and David's five smooth stones. And let's not forget the rainbows—thousands of years' worth of rainbows.

When God declares allegiance to us, He shows us that He means it. The God who loves us is the same one who sets the stars in the night sky and follows winter with spring and night with day. As Scripture says, "The heavens declare the glory of God, and the skies proclaim the work of His hands." If we only open our eyes, we can see all around us proclamations of God's might and declarations of His love.

Some Christians today observe seven sacraments. Others only two. Yet others are simply not into what they call "that whole sacrament thing." Maybe we are all wrong. Whatever we may choose to call them, there are hundreds of signs of God's faithfulness—hundreds of things that can be sacramental if seen through holy eyes.

May you see God's faithfulness in many, many ways and shapes: the comforting hug from a loved one, the melody of a favorite hymn, even the pages of a book. And remember always that *how* God shows His love is not as important as the life-saving fact that God *does* love. That's a promise we can always count on.

I've banked your promises in the vault of my heart.

Psalm 119:11 (MSG)

God Always Has a **Plan B**

for Influencing Friends and Family

*"What the world really needs
is more love and less paperwork."*

Pearl Bailey

Have you ever heard a joke that you just didn't *get*? If you asked the joke-teller for an explanation, chances are that the explanation did not suddenly make the joke funny. Getting a nuts-and-bolts lecture about something—whether it's a joke or the inner workings of a car engine— isn't the same thing as being moved, entertained, or inspired.

As Christian women, we often want to influence our friends, family, and co-workers who don't share our faith. Thus, we collect evidence, counterarguments, Bible verses, and all kinds of other tools to unleash the next time the opportunity arises. We are full of explanations. We are wired for witnessing.

Unfortunately, you can *win* a debate about God and *lose* a chance to draw someone to Him. Many a Christian has laid out an airtight case for her faith, only to hear: "I don't care about all of that. I don't believe in God, no matter what you say about Him. I just don't want to be a Christian."

Faith is often more about the will than the intellect. Jesus didn't say, "I will out-debate everyone so they will have no choice but to believe in me." He said, "I will *draw* everyone to me."

A war of words is unlikely to draw someone to faith or to spark a major change in one's life. But we can each do our part to bring others to our Savior. Love one another. Forgive one another. Work to gain heavenly approval, not mere human approval. Be humble. Be a peacemaker.

People can argue over apologetics, but who can argue with a life lived Jesus' way and the impact that it has? That kind of living has a way of drawing people in the right direction.

*Be kind to one another, tenderhearted, forgiving one another,
as God in Christ forgave you.*

Ephesians 4:32 (RSV)

God Always Has a **Plan B**

for Socking It to Poverty

*"The place God calls you to is the place
your deep gladness and the world's deep hunger meet."*

Frederick Buechner

Have you ever heard the saying about putting yourself in someone else's shoes?

Here is a story about a mom, her four-year-old daughter, and their efforts to put a man in someone else's *socks*.

One Thanksgiving, four-year-old Hannah was helping her mother serve dinner at a rescue mission. Hannah noticed that one of the men standing in the dinner line had shoes but no socks. The day was frigid, and Hannah worried about the man. She voiced her concern to her mom.

"Maybe his shoes will keep his feet warm enough," Hannah's mom offered.

Hannah wasn't so sure. She looked down at her warm, pink socks.

"Mommy," she said, "that man can have *my* socks."

Hannah saw a need and wanted to meet it. She was willing to suffer cold feet so a stranger's feet could be warm. Of course, a preschooler's socks cannot fit a man's feet, but Hannah's suggestion gave her mom an idea.

The next morning, Hannah's mother took her to buy one hundred pairs of new socks to donate to the rescue mission. And that was just the beginning.

Hannah and her mom and dad started a nonprofit organization called Hannah's Socks. Over the past several years, they've provided more than 45,000 pairs of new socks to rescue missions and homeless shelters in Ohio, Hannah's home state.

Sometimes, four-year-olds can be selfish. "Mine!" is one of their favorite words. But Hannah grew up in a generous home. Her mom and dad tried to set a good example of sharing and caring. Hannah heard lots of Bible truths, like Jesus' message, "It is better to give than to receive."

For many of us, every day is like Thanksgiving. We have plenty of clothes—including socks! Refrigerators and pantries are well stocked. We have so many reasons every day to say "Thank you, God!" And one way we can show Him our gratitude is by sharing our blessings with people who don't have as many blessings as we do. Just ask Hannah and her quick-thinking mom.

When a believing person prays, great things happen.

James 5:16 (NCV)

God Always Has a **Plan B**

for Revealing Your True Beauty

"Beauty comes in all ages, colors, shapes, and forms. God never makes junk."

Kathy Ireland

If you've recently stepped on the scale and cringed at the numbers, perhaps you should consider moving to Mauritania.

In this West African country, you see, it's believed that the more a woman weighs, the better her chance of securing a husband.

Meanwhile, along the border of Thailand and Burma, a long neck is considered attractive—a really, really long neck. Women begin this "beauty treatment" as young girls by stacking more and more heavy metal bands around their necks. By the time they reach adulthood, these women have weakened the muscles in their elongated necks so much that removing the bands would cause them to suffocate.

In Ethiopia, scars are made by cutting into a woman's stomach to enhance her beauty.

The Maori women of New Zealand cover their lips and chins with blue tattoos.

One might think that American beauty standards are more reasonable, but even those standards have shifted dramatically. In the 1700s, pear-shaped hips were considered attractive. (So was shaving your eyebrows and replacing them with ones made of press-on mouse skin!)

In the 1800s, women were encouraged to look frail and pale. In the 1920s, women bound their chests to have more boyish figures.

When it comes to measuring one's worth, appearance is always part of the equation. And for centuries, women (and men) have gone to extremes to meet the current standards of beauty. In some cases, that is not enough. Some women just *have* to rise above the current standard. They demand the biggest breasts, the tightest abs, and the best hair.

In reality, each person is like a single piece in a giant jigsaw puzzle that stretches through time. We're all different shapes and colors, each filling a unique spot that helps complete the final picture. You may be an eye-catching flower petal on a begonia, a burst of lava from an erupting volcano, or a gleaming tooth on a Bengal tiger.

Or you may be one of those blue pieces of sky. You know, the ones that, at first glance, all seem to look alike. But try to put one piece of sky into the spot designed for another piece and what happens? It won't fit.

You can try jamming it in, pounding it down, or bending the corners up a bit. But even if you succeed in forcing that piece into a spot where it doesn't belong, it will never look quite right. And somewhere else in the puzzle there will be a hole in the picture—a spot where that now-mangled piece would have fit just perfectly.

Every piece plays its part. And every person plays her part. Sometimes it takes a while to find your part, your special spot. That's part of the adventure of being a woman. No matter your age, you're still discovering who you are and where you fit—what part of the big picture you were created to fill. That process involves trial and error, just like working any puzzle with dozens and dozens of pieces. That means you can feel free to try out for the community theater, see if playing guitar is your thing, or start writing a blog. You can feel equally proud of being a performer, a budding musician, or a humor writer.

If you're searching for a standard by which to measure yourself, forget about comparing yourself against others—physically or any other way. Every time you compare yourself with another piece of the puzzle, you lose sight of how truly valuable that one-of-a-kind *you* really is. You lose sight of your true worth.

It's like comparing apples to oranges or blue sky to blue sea.

If you must compare, compare who you are *trying* to be with who you believe you truly are, in your heart and soul. If something is off there, pray that God can get you back on the right path.

Remember, no one can ever be a better you than *you*.

You created my inmost being;
you knit me together in my mother's womb.
I praise you because I am
fearfully and wonderfully made.

Psalms 139:13-14

God Always Has a **Plan B**

for Helping You Live On Purpose

"Pray hard, work hard, and leave the rest to God."

Florence Griffith-Joyner

From birth, it seemed that Wilma Rudolph could not seem to catch a break. She was the twentieth of twenty-two children born into an African-American family in Tennessee. Known as "the sickliest child in all of Clarksville," Willie suffered through measles, mumps, chicken pox, double pneumonia, and scarlet fever. At age four, she contracted polio, which paralyzed her left leg.

At five, Willie began wearing a metal leg brace. Her poor health prevented her from attending kindergarten or first grade, so she began school in the second grade. In her autobiography, Willie explained that she attended a segregated school, but her red hair and light skin, along with her leg brace, made her feel like an outsider, even among her peers.

Willie's father was a railroad porter. Her mother worked as a maid. Even with a grueling work schedule and a large family, Willie's parents and siblings faithfully helped her strengthen her weak leg with physical therapy four times a day, three to four days a week. One Sunday at church, eleven-year-old Willie removed her brace and proudly walked unassisted down the center aisle. Her family looked on, glowing with pride.

At thirteen, Willie got involved in organized sports at school. Like her sister Yolanda, Willie joined the basketball team. But Willie rode the bench for three years, seeing zero court time. In year four of her high school basketball career, Willie finally saw game action. There, she was spotted by a college coach who invited her to attend a summer, multisport camp. At that camp, Willie tried running track.

Soon Willie was not only running track but winning every race she ran. At age twenty, "the sickliest child in Clarksville" became known as "the fastest woman alive." At the 1960 Olympic Games, Willie won the 100-meter dash, the 200-meter dash, and the 400-meter relay. She became the first American woman to win three gold medals during one Olympics, matching the accomplishment of her personal hero, Olympic legend Jesse Owens.

When Willie returned home to Clarksville, the city proposed a parade in her honor—a racially segregated parade. Willie refused to participate unless everyone, regardless of race, could take part. Thus, her hometown celebration became the city's first racially integrated event.

Soon, Willie said she believed God had greater things for her to do than win medals. She was right. The fastest woman alive retired from running in 1962 and became a second-grade teacher and high school coach. Later, she founded the Wilma Rudolph Foundation to help disadvantaged young athletes discover their true potential. She also traveled with Billy Graham and the Baptist Christian Athletes, inspiring people all over the world with her story.

"But wait!" cynics might say. "Not everyone who wants to walk *will* walk. Not everyone who trains hard will win an Olympic gold medal, no matter how many years she puts in."

That's true. But Willie's medals are not the most important part of her story. They simply brought her amazing life to the attention of the world. Back when Willie was a kid, her goal wasn't to win a medal and become an Olympic legend. Willie didn't even hear of the Olympics until she was sixteen. Long before she began running, Willie's goal was simple—to see if she could walk. This was something doctors doubted she would do. Yet, Willie reached her goal, literally, one step at a time. Olympic gold was just a bonus.

Willie's true competition was never other runners. She was competing against herself and learning to accept herself and her challenges. When it came to self-acceptance, she had a choice: resignation or celebration. She chose celebration. When she was ill and frail, Willie saw beyond who she was at the moment to who she believed she could be—who she believed God had created her to be. Then, she did what she could to help herself go, and grow, in that direction.

Just like Willie, your life story is written one day at a time. You may be facing tough challenges. You may struggle with disadvantages, disabilities, or discouragement. You may not have the support of a husband or boyfriend. But you're not alone. There's someone pulling for you, someone who knows you inside and out. Someone who understands your place in the big picture and knows exactly where the puzzle piece that is "you" belongs. He wants to help you see yourself through His eyes. He wants you to know you're so much more precious than gold to Him.

*It's in Christ
that we find out who we are
and what we're living for.*

Ephesians 1:11 (MSG)

God Always Has a **Plan B**

for Finding a "Do" in Every "Don't"

*"God gives us the ingredients for our daily bread,
but he expects us to do the baking."*

William Arthur Ward

Why did God give us such a long list of rules to follow? Why is the Bible jam-packed with "thou shalt nots"? Is God some kind of egomaniac who created people just so He would have somebody to push around? Wouldn't life be simpler without all those commandments?

Look at it this way: Why doesn't a mother let her toddler touch a hot stove? Why doesn't a teacher let her kids spend recess on a busy street instead of the playground? Why does a doctor insist on having a patient's medical history before she prescribes medication?

In each of the above examples, the rules might be quite frustrating to the person required to obey them.

A toddler wants to touch the stove because the orange glow is alluring. School kids might want to play in the street because the same old playground has become boring and they want to flirt with danger. And a sick person wants medication right now—no questions asked! The background check is just more "red tape." It's a roadblock on the path to healing.

At the moment each of these people collides with a brick wall called "Rules," the first instinct is to get around, over, under, or through that troublesome wall.

Little thought is given to the fact that the rules are meant to protect, to ensure safety and happiness.

Similarly, abiding by our Creator's commandments ensures our protection, fulfillment, peace, and well-being. The quality of our lives is a product of our choices, and we don't always have the information, wisdom, or perspective to make the best choices. That's precisely why the God who loves us and yearns to see us succeed has given us rules to live by.

Besides, at their core, even the commandments that begin with "don't" or "thou shalt not" are positive. For example, "don't covet" is another way of saying DO appreciate what you have. Be grateful for it. Get true joy from it by avoiding comparing your stuff with someone else's.

"Don't kill" means DO value and treasure life—yours and that of others. DO realize that God created every person with the capacity to do good in the world. Be aware of the evil inherent in maliciously robbing another human being of his or her life, potential, and dreams. "Thou shalt not steal" is another way of saying thou SHALT respect others' property. If you want more possessions, more money, more whatever, go out and earn it.

If you have been viewing the Ten Commandments or other biblical rules as a big stick God uses to beat His creation into submission, it's time to shift your perspective. God is for you, not against you.

How blessed you are to have a Lord and Savior who cares enough to provide rules to help you achieve the "abundant life" Jesus promised.

Your word is a lamp to my feet and a light for my path.

Psalms 119:105 (NKJV)

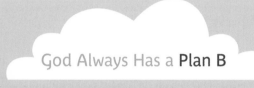

God Always Has a **Plan B**

for Making Second Acts Shine

How late is *too* late to do something great in life? To make a major change that makes all the difference in the world?

Before you answer, consider this story.

A seventy-eight-year-old woman decided to take up painting. Not houses but canvases. She had never had an art lesson. In fact, she had never stepped inside an art gallery.

She had almost no formal education, and she had spent almost fifty years as a hired hand on a farm. The decades of hard work had given her arthritis.

And yet, at age seventy-eight, she decided to take up painting.

Ten years later she was one of the best known and best loved artists in the world. By the time she reached ninety, the galleries displaying her work outnumbered the candles on her birthday cake. Among her birthday cards that year were greetings from four US presidents.

This late-bloomer passed away in 1961 at age 101. She had spent almost a quarter of a century as a world-class artist. Every major newspaper and news magazine in the country featured tributes and retrospectives. From across the world, various heads of state sent their condolences to her family.

The painter's name, as you have probably surmised, is Grandma Moses.

When asked how she decided to become a painter, she said, "I decided to quit existing and start *living*." In other words, she set a new goal for her life. She thought about who she truly was, what she wanted to become, and how to get there.

So the next time you fear it's too late to realize your dreams, think of Grandma Moses. The painting of your life isn't complete until you say it's complete.

"For I know the plans I have for you,"
declares the LORD,
"plans to prosper you and not to harm you,
plans to give you a hope and a future.
Then you will call upon me
and come and pray to me,
and I will listen to you.
You will seek me and find me
when you seek me with all your heart."

Jeremiah 29:11-13

God Always Has a **Plan B**

for Rewarding Clean Living

"I feel responsible to be a role model for younger kids. That's important to me. I hope that people can distinguish my character and the way I present myself."

Allyson Felix

The high school track coach stared at his stopwatch in disbelief. There was no way a skinny ninth-grader, wearing clunky basketball shoes, could run so fast. So the coach asked Allyson Felix to run again.

Stopwatches don't lie, especially not twice. Thus, the coach realized the truth: his new freshman phenom, who'd never even worn a pair of track shoes, was a once-in-a-generation talent.

Young Allyson went on to make it to the California state finals during her first year of competition. The following season, she won the state title in the 100 meters. By the time she was a junior, she was running in large international meets against the world's best sprinters. Despite being several years younger—and much slighter of build—than her elite completion, Allyson left most of the world's fastest women in her wake.

At eighteen, she won the 200 meters silver medal at the 2004

Olympics, breaking the world junior record in the process. One year later, she captured first place at the world championships of track and field.

She would dominate sprinting events for the next two years, always humble in victory. She shunned the fist-pumping, chest-thumping, and muscle-flexing that often comes with the territory in both men's and women's sprinting.

Allyson entered the 2008 Olympics in Beijing as the clear favorite for the gold medal in the 200 meters. She ran well through the qualifying rounds, but she hit the wall in the finals and finished second again. She was clearly disappointed but handled the postrace scene with grace.

She credited her family with "putting everything into perspective." She added that the high profile of events like the Olympics means that "everyone is watching you and everything that you do, so [you] feel like that's your best opportunity to show what you're really about."

But as Allyson evolved from teen sensation to veteran athlete, she decided she needed to do more than demonstrate maturity and grace in the crucible of world-class competition.

For decades, US track and field has dragged behind it the ugly baggage of illegal performance-enhancing drugs. Steroid use resulted in multiple disqualifications—and even jail time—for American sprinter Marion Jones, one of the most celebrated track stars of the past generation. Other sprinters have faced suspensions, had national and world-record times revoked, and been forced to return medals they won.

Tired of the cloud of suspicion hovering above her sport, Allyson declared a low-key but public war. She submitted to an array of random tests, which were both inconvenient and unpleasant for such a quiet, private person. The tests were risky, too. A mix-up or sabotage in the testing lab could derail an innocent athlete's career.

But Allyson was determined to restore credibility to her sport and to demonstrate the values her family instilled in her.

"Whatever I can do to prove I'm clean, I'm willing," she states, "no matter what time I have to wake up or where I have to drive for testing. I feel responsible to be a role model for younger kids. That's important to me. I hope that people can distinguish my character and the way I present myself."

Allyson Felix presented herself quite well at the 2012 London Olympic Games. Running clean (and fast) she won three gold medals, including one in that pesky 200 meters.

*Do not conform any longer
to the pattern of this world,
but be transformed
by the renewing of your mind.*

Romans 12:2

God Always Has a **Plan B**

for Handling Success
(It's harder than you think)

"A lot of life is Plan B."

Anne Lamott

Former Olympic skier Picabo Street has an intriguing perspective on her success: "Having *won* an Olympic gold medal—a dream since age eleven—was harder than *trying* to win it," she says.

The insight seems odd at first, but it makes more sense upon deeper reflection. After all, mountains of books have been written about facing failure, but how many books offer guidance on the pitfalls of how we handle *success*?

There would be a ready market for such books. How many times have headlines proclaimed the woes of superstars in various fields (sports, politics, entertainment, or high finance) who have self-destructed after realizing lifelong dreams? In the aftermath of their success, they feel lost, as if they've been on a bullet train traveling 200 miles an hour—only to come to an abrupt stop. Sure, they indulge in the requisite "victory tours" and photo-ops, but soon they are haunted by frightening questions:

"What if this is the high point of my life and nothing else in the decades that come will compare?"

"What's next? How do I top *this*?"

"Do the people hanging around me genuinely care about me, or do they all want something from me?"

"Do I need to recreate this experience to have any chance of being happy again?"

Now, you probably are not going to win an Olympic gold medal or become the next American Idol. But chances are that you will enjoy achievement in life, maybe even a major achievement in your chosen field. And, like Picabo Street, you'll be faced with your own "What now?" questions. And the way you answer those questions will make a big difference in your life.

We've all seen the mistakes: The actress who stars in a blockbuster and is so eager to recreate the buzz that she hastily takes a role in a flop, damaging her credibility and drawing ridicule from the press and from her fans. Or the athlete who tries to keep playing despite the ravages of age and injury and ends up embarrassing himself or causing permanent physical damage.

In Picabo Street's case, less than two weeks after winning a super-G gold medal in the Winter Olympics, she hurried off to the World Cup races in Switzerland. During her downhill race, she crashed, breaking her left leg and blowing out her right knee. The surgery and requisite recovery gobbled up almost two years of her life.

What drove Picabo to race again so quickly after her Olympic triumph? The belief that "the only way to top a gold medal was to win two." In retrospect, she acknowledges that she should have taken more time to enjoy her achievement and *then* thoughtfully and carefully set her next goals.

The lesson here: Be open to having a "second act" in life. And note that success in that act might look different from that of Act One.

For some, that means leaving a high-speed business career for something different, like coaching a high school baseball team or becoming a parent. Former President Jimmy Carter is a prime example of this principle. After leaving the White House, he founded the Carter Center, a nonprofit organization that advances human rights and helps fight disease, especially in Asia and Africa. He also became a key figure in Habitat for Humanity, which provides homes for needy people.

And, as if that were not enough, he has also written best-selling books, both fiction and nonfiction.

Success in one discipline doesn't need to limit or define you any more than failure does. The truly happy person isn't addicted to success in one chosen field. She enjoys it and appreciates it, but then, when it's time, she moves on to *new* quests for success.

*I've learned by now to be quite content
whatever my circumstances.
I'm just as happy
with little as with much.*

Philippians 4:10 (MSG)

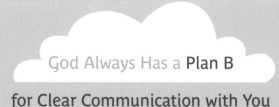

God Always Has a **Plan B**

for Clear Communication with You

*"It's not about religion;
it's about relationship."*

R. Alan Woods

The God of the entire universe longs to communicate with *you*! Let that truth sink in for a moment. It's amazing but true.

Many of us would consider it the opportunity of a lifetime to, just once, talk with a favorite recording artist, athlete, CEO, or movie star. We would be eager to tell our girlfriends or our sweetie about our "brush with greatness," knowing that they would be impressed (and probably jealous).

Unfortunately, we don't always show the same zeal for communicating with God, who loves us, who is far more fascinating than any person we could ever encounter, and who longs to fellowship with us.

God created the universe and everything in it—including the big shots we revere. He created us to have a relationship with Him. And the only way to have a relationship with anyone is to spend time with him or her. With God, this time can include prayer, meditation, reading the Bible or Christian books, listening to music, and worship.

Think about it: What relationship is more important than your personal relationship with God? Who is more worth knowing? After all, God created you, He loves you, and He has all the answers. What's more, your bond with him forms the foundation for all other relationships.

The Lord of all creation is waiting for you. You might not know Him well, but He knows you. He wants to hear from you. There is no risk. God will never betray your relationship with Him. So don't wait another second. Open your eyes; open your heart. God wants to communicate with you right now!

Remember, even if you have neglected your relationship with God, He still yearns to be close to you. He holds no grudges. Instead, He holds His people close at heart.

The LORD God then said:
I will look for my sheep
and take care of them myself.

Ezekiel 34:11 (CEV)

God Always Has a **Plan B**

for Helping You Keep Your Promises

Carrie Lakey and her husband, Jimmy, had planned to adopt a child someday, but when they were asked to lead a group of college students on a short-term mission trip to Rwanda, they realized that *someday* might be imminent. So, in the months leading up to the trip, they prayed to God saying, "We will knock on doors, and as long as the doors keep opening, we will keep going. If not, we will know [adoption] is for another time."

Surprisingly, given the complicated world of international adoption, the doors remained open throughout the long process. More surprising still, when Carrie and Jimmy looked separately through the pictures of the children they might adopt, they both chose the same shy young boy with his finger in his mouth.

At every juncture of the process, the Lakeys felt God leading them to this boy. They eventually learned that this child had been found abandoned in a drainage culvert during an evening rainstorm in the Gikondo District of Kigali, Rwanda.

Their hearts went out to him, and they continued to pursue his adoption.

When they first saw the young boy named River at an orphanage outside of Kigali, he was playing with about fifty other children on the dusty lot that served as a playground. The Lakeys couldn't reveal their intentions to River because the other children would be jealous.

As the Lakeys stood with the orphanage director and scanned the playground full of all the other children they would *not* be taking home with them, Carrie and Jimmy had a revelation. These children that their son-to-be would soon be leaving behind were his friends, the closest thing he had known to a family.

The Lakeys wanted to do something for these kids, so they asked the director what the children's greatest need was. They expected him to say food and clothing, something they could address with a simple cash donation.

But the director's answer surprised them: "School fees."

"But don't you have public education here?" Jimmy asked.

"Yes, but there are still school fees we must pay or the children cannot attend," the director explained.

"Well, how much is a school fee?" Carrie wondered. "And is that really more important than food and clothes?"

The director turned and looked the couple in the eyes for the first time since the conversation started. "Look at these children," he said. "They are clothed OK, and we feed them OK—not great, but it is OK. But we cannot send them to school because of the fees. And without school, they will have nothing."

Carrie and Jimmy asked about the exact cost of the school fees. The director answered, giving the total in Rwandan francs.

After doing the math, the Lakeys were convinced the figure was far too low. Could $1.93 a week really send a child to school?

The answer was yes. School tuition was only about $100 a year.

That evening, as Carrie and Jimmy talked about what they had learned that day, they imagined how River, when he was older, would one day look back at the pictures of his homeland and wonder about what had happened to the rest of the boys and girls he had left behind. They imagined him asking them why they had chosen to do something for him and not the rest of those children. They realized that without education, there was little hope of these children growing up to break free from the grip of poverty.

As the couple talked, they agreed that they wanted to be able to look their son in the eye and say, "River, we did everything we could for your earliest friends. If nothing else, we sent them all to school."

Carrie and Jimmy looked at their budget. They would have to make some sacrifices in their lifestyle, but they could cover the cost of educating fifty of the hundred orphans.

However, when the couple returned home and talked to family and friends about "the orphan project," they learned that these people wanted to help. River would grow up in their community, they said, and they would be part of his larger support system. But they wanted to help his friends as well.

Over and over, the Lakeys heard, "You've made a promise to River to help these kids. We want to keep that promise, too. What can we do?"

As more and more people asked that question, Carrie and Jimmy felt they should formalize the effort. Calling it "the orphan project" didn't make sense anymore. So, as they put their heads together with others, they decided to call their nonprofit venture to help these Rwandan children River's Promise (www.riverspromise.com).

Jimmy works as a concert promoter, so now River's face is often seen alongside that of top artists on concert promotional materials. Several artist friends of Carrie and Jimmy banded together to record a CD and used the proceeds to help fulfill River's Promise.

In a matter of months, the effort raised enough money to send all of the children at the orphanage to school. So the Lakeys inquired about other needs. When they found out that River's old friends were sleeping on cement floors, they bought them beds with mosquito netting.

After the 2010 earthquake in Haiti, River's Promise sent money to help orphans there.

Carrie and Jimmy are amazed at all that has happened since they decided to adopt River. At this writing, River Lakey is in the middle of his fourth year living in the United States. He is adapting well to his new culture. It is hard to find him without a smile beaming on his face. He certainly loves having Carrie and Jimmy Lakey as his family. But his family also extends to everyone around him, people who continue to fulfill the promise to educate and care for his friends back in Rwanda.

Looking back on all that has happened, Carrie says it was a case of God sneaking up on her and her husband and putting a sense of mission in their hearts—a mission they never dreamed of, but one they wouldn't trade for anything. The Lakeys believe their story shows the power of following God one step at a time and what can happen when you walk through the doors He opens for you.

He called a little child to him, and placed the child among them. And he said: "Truly I tell you, unless you change and become like little children, you will never enter the kingdom of heaven. Therefore, whoever takes the lowly position of this child is the greatest in the kingdom of heaven. And whoever welcomes one such child in my name welcomes me."

Matthew 18:2-5

God Always Has a **Plan B**

for Helping You Love Your Enemies (and "Frenemies")

*"People may sometimes doubt what you say,
but they will always believe what you do."*

American Proverb

Of all the Bible's commandments, perhaps none is tougher than "Love your enemies." Not tolerate them or do them a few favors just to show what a stellar woman you are. No, Jesus said to *love* them. Those hateful, cruel, dishonest people. The neighbor who spreads hurtful rumors about you. The so-called friend who backstabs you. The boss who just won't give you a break. The ex who just can't seem to let bygones be bygones.

Loving an enemy is a hard, often unpleasant task. That's why prayer is the first step in the process. Pray that you'll have the grace, the will, and the patience to show love. Pray that your enemy will accept your efforts and goodwill.

You might also need to pray about your own bitterness. That way, even if your prayers don't change an enemy's ugly qualities, they will still change *you*.

As you pray for your enemies and try to bring peace to your relationships with them, you might come to realize that these people are no less attractive to God or loved by Him than you are. Further, as you experience what hard work it is to love unlovable people, you might appreciate anew God's love for you.

Yes, dealing with enemies is hard. But if you reach out in love to a difficult person in your life, you can reduce your list of enemies by one, and, perhaps, gain a friend at the same time.

I tell you, love your enemies.
Help and give without expecting a return.
You'll never—I promise—regret it.

Luke 6:35 (MSG)

God Always Has a **Plan B**

for Playing Life By Ear

*"The greatest good you can do for others is
not just to share your riches
but to reveal to them their own."*

Benjamin Disraeli

Want to do something really kind and meaningful for the people in your life? Listen to them. Really listen. Women are traditionally known as better listeners than men, but even we can fall into the mode of robotically nodding our heads and muttering "Uh-huh" as we wait for *our* turn to talk. Truly listening means thinking about the words that are being said and the body language that accompanies them.

People today are bombarded with messages. Voices ring out everywhere. Everyone talks. Few truly listen. Whether it's your friends, neighbors, relatives, or, yes, even your husband or boyfriend, your willingness to listen to them can be one of the greatest gifts you can give. It's a profound way to show you truly care.

Want an example? In the 1800s, two powerful men vied for political leadership of Great Britain. Both William Gladstone and Benjamin Disraeli were intelligent, successful, and important men. However, Disraeli had a distinct advantage that was best expressed by a thoughtful woman who happened to dine with the two statesmen on consecutive evenings.

Her assessment of Gladstone: "When I left the dining room after sitting next to Mister Gladstone, I thought he was the cleverest man in England."

Following her dinner with Disraeli, however, she said, "After sitting next to Mister Disraeli, I thought *I* was the cleverest woman in England!"

Many people today are obsessed with proving how clever and important they are. You can stand apart from the crowd and make a difference in the lives of those around you by abstaining from all the self-promotion and lending an ear (better yet, two ears) in an effort to make others feel valued and important.

As Disraeli himself understood, "The greatest good you can do for others is not just to share your riches but to reveal to them their own."

Love from the center of who you are; don't fake it. . . .
Be good friends who love deeply;
practice playing second fiddle.

Romans 12:9-10 (MSG)

God Always Has a **Plan B**

for Making You Passionate About Compassion

*"Would that Christ would teach my soul a prayer
that would plead to the Father for grace sufficient for you."*

Clara Barton

Of the many great women in American history, few are as admirable as Clara Barton. She began her career as a teacher at age fifteen. And this was in 1836, when almost all teachers were men (and not teenage men).

Later in life, in her forties, she served as a nurse in the Civil War, sometimes risking her life in the heat of battle to tend to the wounded. Her courage, expertise, and grace earned her the title "Angel of the Battlefield." She didn't just tend to soldiers' wounds. She read to them, wrote letters for them, listened to their concerns and stories, and prayed with them.

After the war ended, she worked to reunite injured soldiers with their families.

At age sixty, she founded the American Red Cross, which she led for twenty-three years, never drawing a salary.

At this point, you might be wondering: "What was Clara Barton's secret for success? How was she able to serve others so well?" You might be surprised to learn that her secret is a quality you possess and one you can build upon.

The hallmark of Barton's life was compassion. This word comes from the Latin stems *com* (with) and *pati* (suffer). Compassionate people suffer with others. They take others' pain and grief as their own.

Barton displayed her compassion at an early age. When she was eleven, her older brother David was seriously injured when he fell from the rafters while building a barn. For two years, Clara helped care for David, developing the skills and patience that would serve her on the battlefield many years later.

Even though she worked on some of the Civil War's bloodiest battlefields, she didn't feel that her service was anything extraordinary. "While our soldiers can stand and fight," she said matter-of-factly, "I can stand and feed and nurse them. You must never so much as think if you like it or not, if it is bearable or not. You must never think of anything but the need and how to meet it."

We can't all serve on the battlefield or start huge organizations. But we can all be like Clara Barton by being compassionate people who see needs and try our best to meet them.

Never walk away from someone who deserves help;
your hand is God's hand for that person.

Proverbs 3:27 (MSG)

God Always Has a **Plan B**

for Helping You Lead Others to Succeed

"A leader is someone who can give correction without causing resentment."

Coach John Wooden

Walking through a heavily wooded national park, a woman noticed a crooked tree. It looked like a lowercase letter "r." She noticed that near the tree someone had placed a large upright pole and tied it to the tree with ropes. Clearly, this was an attempt to straighten out the crooked tree as it grew.

However, the woman noted that the upper part of the tree had already veered quite far from its base. Nothing was going to correct the misdirected growth. The crooked part of the tree was too far from the corrective pole.

This story carries a lesson for today's woman. No matter your situation, you are probably a leader of some sort—a parent, coach, manager, community organizer, or head of a committee at your church or civic organization. As a leader, you have a responsibility to guide those you lead. But it's hard to correct and redirect people, whether they are your kids, someone else's kids, your employees, or the folks on the church finance committee.

After all, who wants to hurt someone's feelings, or risk harming a relationship? Unfortunately, those risks are part of being a leader. As a leader, you must keep people and projects on track. That means regular and consistent feedback, even when that feedback is not all sunshine and rainbows.

Otherwise, people and projects can veer off course. And, like that tree, the longer problems go unchecked, the harder it is to correct them.

If you struggle with giving what some business consultants call "negative feedback," consider this: You do people a *favor* when you set clear expectations for them. Without such expectations, how can someone know if he or she is succeeding?

When you have to correct or discipline someone, emphasize that your words and actions show that you *care*. You care enough to keep someone on the right path and moving at the right speed.

With prayer, care, and tact, a strong woman leader can help others grow to become all they can be.

Rebuke the wise and they will love you.
Instruct the wise and they will be wiser still.

Proverbs 9:8-9 (NIV)

God Always Has a **Plan B**

for Helping You Be *Simply* Successful

"For the beautiful word begets the beautiful deed."

Thomas Mann

Too often, the life of a twenty-first-century woman is anything but simple. In reality, our days, weeks, months, and years can become a tornado of busy schedules, interpersonal conflicts, and to-do lists that never get to-done. It seems that most of our lives can be spent somewhere in between problems and opportunities—not knowing which to attack first.

Indeed, think of how much of life is "in between"—in between things like meetings, conference calls, medical appointments, errand-running, and home repairs (whether we are doing the repairing or waiting on the "experts").

There must be a more simple way to navigate this busy thing called life.

Writer Linda Ellis, author of popular long-form poem *The Dash*, says the key is living to make a difference. She contends: "It's not the date you were born or the date you died that really matters. It's 'the dash' between those years and what you do with it—to make a difference with your life."

Are we truly making a difference? Sometimes we need to hit the pause button to answer this question correctly. We need to slow down and think. We need to ask: "What are the things in my life that feed and inspire me? And what should I be doing to feed, inspire, and serve others? What can I say to them? What can I do for them?"

The answers to these questions give us perspective. They can even give us energy as we see more clearly the finish line for another leg of the race called life. Yes, some of the mundane tasks still need to be done, but perhaps there is a way to do them with kindness and creativity and patience. For example, maybe that dreaded weekly meeting is a chance to tell a co-worker how much you appreciate her expertise or even her smile.

At the end of the day, it's the simple little things—the simple little actions and the simple little words—that constitute so much of life. They keep us going. They help us keep *others* going.

True, life is busy sometimes. Life is complicated sometimes. But with the right perspective and sense of purpose, it *can* be simpler—and more simply rewarding.

What does the Lord require of you?
To act justly and to love mercy
and to walk humbly with your God.

Micah 6:8 (NIV)

God Always Has a **Plan B**

for Reordering Priorities

*"The Lord stands above the new day,
for God has made it.
All restlessness, all worry and anxiety
flee before him."*

Dietrich Bonhoeffer

One day, a hardworking single mom received the following e-mail from her eighteen-year-old daughter, who was halfway through her first year in college, hundreds of miles away:

Hi, Mom,

Hey, I have some big news for you. I have fallen in love with a man who is several years my senior. Twenty-two years senior, to be exact. He is one of the custodians here at school. While he never finished high school, he is a great dad to his two kids, one of whom is almost my exact same age! What a coincidence, huh?

Of course, because his job doesn't pay very well, I am quitting school to work as a server in a bar near campus. I need to get some money socked away before the wedding! Speaking of which, we haven't set a date yet. That will depend on whether or not I am pregnant.

The mother felt her eyes filling with tears. She wasn't sure if they were tears of anger, grief, or some of each. She blinked away the tears and continued reading:

OK, Mom, I hope you know by now that none of what I have written is true. There's no boyfriend, no impending wedding, and no chance I am quitting school. However, it does look like I might get a D in freshman composition. And I could really use a little extra money to help pay for gas. It's really expensive here. Thanks for everything you do for me!

That day, a freshman student taught her mother a valuable lesson: Perspective is all-important. Sometimes, the things we think are "troubles" are not truly troubles at all.

Be patient with each other, making allowance for each other's faults because of your love.

Ephesians 4:2 (NLT)

God Always Has a **Plan B**

for Making Small Blessings Add Up

"God's gifts put man's best dreams to shame."

Elizabeth Barrett Browning

This morning, did your own private robot roll into your bedroom and wake you up by playing some of your favorite songs on his onboard, high-tech sound system?

Did a famous TV chef cook your breakfast?

The last time you took a trip, did you travel by private helicopter or stretch limousine?

If you are like most women, the answer to all of these questions is "No." (Or, "I wish!") But a life without a lot of fancy and expensive stuff can still be amazing. Really. Every day, God provides dozens of small blessings, blessings that can be enjoyed by anyone with the eyes to see them and the hearts to appreciate them: the warmth of that special someone's smile, watching a favorite TV show or movie with a couple of close friends, the beauty of a sunset, hearing "Great work!" from a boss or co-worker, or the comfort of crawling into bed after a busy, busy day.

Always remember that enjoying God's small blessings can make a so-called common life uncommonly good. The difference between an ordinary life and an extraordinary one is the "extra" care we take to appreciate all the ways God shows He cares for us.

*Make sure that your character
is free from the love of money,
being content with what you have.*

Hebrews 13:5 (NASB)

God Always Has a **Plan B**

for Honoring Sincere Effort

"Every calling is great when greatly pursued."

Oliver Wendell Holmes Jr.

A teenage girl visited her biological mother one summer and (reluctantly) accompanied Mom to church in a small farm community. As the pastor stood at the pulpit and began his sermon, the teen thought: "This guy is the worst preacher I've ever heard. He isn't funny or insightful like my pastor back home. He doesn't have a very good speaking voice. And he looks nervous and uncomfortable up there."

The girl sat bored and discouraged for the next twenty minutes, wishing her mother had let her bring the smartphone or, better yet, let her stay home and sleep in. She sighed with relief when she heard the words "And in conclusion . . ."

"Thank goodness that's over," she thought cynically. Then, she heard a faint sniffling sound and turned to a woman sitting next to her. The woman was sobbing quietly and dabbing her eyes with a tattered tissue. "That was just what I needed to hear," she said, her voice ringing with gratitude and sincerity.

The teen's mom nodded sympathetically and gave the woman a fresh tissue from her purse.

The teen swallowed hard, feeling a bit guilty. But she learned a valuable lesson that day: through God's grace and provision, a message that might lack in style can still speak to the hearts of listeners.

Have you ever been afraid to write a poem, draw a picture, give a speech, or sing a song because you thought your talents weren't worthy of anyone's attention? If so, take heart. God doesn't expect you to be polished and perfect in your endeavors. He's not going to compare your efforts with someone else's. He just expects you to be sincere and faithful. And if you simply do your best, your efforts can touch hearts.

It's substance, not style, that will make your efforts to minister to others successful.

*Laugh with your happy friends
when they're happy.
Share tears when they're down.
Get along with each other;
don't be stuck-up.
Make friends with nobodies;
don't be the great somebody.*

Romans 12:15-16 (MSG)

God Always Has a **Plan B**

for Blessing Those Who Persevere

Sally didn't want to be a TV star. She just wanted to be on the radio, a correspondent or a disc jockey. She didn't have to be seen, as long as she could be heard.

However, the recent college grad could not find any radio station in the entire United States that would hire her. "No woman can attract a radio audience," she was told over and over.

So she broadened her search. She made her way to the Dominican Republic, where she found work as a radio reporter covering political uprisings.

With some experience on her résumé, Sally returned to the United States to try her luck again. She did find radio jobs this time. The problem was *keeping* those radio jobs. She was fired from eighteen stations. Things were so rough at one point that Sally found herself living in her car.

After firing number eighteen, Sally took stock of her life. She knew she wanted a life in broadcasting, but she wondered if she had the skills and personality for it. And she wondered if radio really was too much of a man's world.

What's more, she was now in her late forties. Time was running short. It was hard enough for a woman to make it in radio; the odds were stacked against a *middle-aged* woman.

Then she heard about a job opening: host of a political talk show.

Sally knew virtually nothing about politics. Still, she convinced the show's executives to give her a chance. Using her low-key, conversational style, she hosted her first episode, sharing what the July 4 holiday meant to her. She didn't speak from a vast knowledge of politics; she spoke from her heart. Then she invited listeners to call in and do the same.

The phone lines jammed. The show was an instant hit.

Within two years, Sally Jesse Raphael's radio talk show had moved to television, where it reached more than eight million viewers in North America and the United Kingdom. For the next two decades, viewers tuned in to hear what the woman with the easy style and oversized, red-framed glasses had to say.

During the course of the Emmy-winning show's long run, Sally had plenty of chances to encourage her viewers to use every setback and failure to spur them on to something better, just as she had done.

She also insisted that a sense of humor is vital for enduring those hardships. She quipped, "You go to college, you get a master's degree, you study Shakespeare . . . and you wind up being famous for plastic glasses. Go figure."

Spoken like a woman who knows that one must face life's challenges with clear eyes (bespectacled though they may be), not through rose-colored glasses.

Whatever you do, work at it with all your heart,
as working for the Lord, not for human masters.

Colossians 3:23

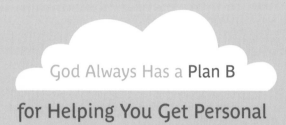

God Always Has a **Plan B**

for Helping You Get Personal

A huge gap, a Grand Canyon, stands between knowing about God and truly *knowing* Him. For many of us, God is like a movie. We've read the reviews, seen the previews. We can summarize the plot, even quote a line or two of dialogue. We can even form a thumbs-up or thumbs-down opinion. But we haven't actually seen the film.

Or, God is like an exotic destination somewhere. We've seen the brochures, maybe even the informational DVD. The place sure looks great. But we've never been there.

God is your loving creator, and He wants you to experience Him firsthand. So read His book. Listen to His music. Hear His modern-day prophets (pastors, youth pastors, singers, authors, and musicians).

Take time to simply be still in God's presence and ask Him to fill your head and your heart with His love.

Further, don't let your prayers become obligatory quick monologues to God or long wish lists. Make them conversations with him.

To have a close, rewarding relationship with God, you don't have to be perfect. But you do need to be genuinely committed to the relationship. Just as a woman can't be "mostly married" or "somewhat pregnant," you cannot have a "sort of" relationship with God. A relationship with the all-loving, all-powerful God of the universe just doesn't work that way. Being close to God includes spending time with him at His house, with His people. Making time to worship. Time to praise. Time to support and be supported by other believers.

If you avoid church or let your Bible gather dust on a shelf, will God still love you? Of course. He loved you long before you were even aware of Him. He loved you before the first church was built or the first word of the Bible was penned. But if you truly want to grow close to God, to return even a portion of the love He has showered on you, you need to spend time with Him. Why not start today?

See how very much our Father loves us,
for he calls us his children.

1 John 3:1 (NLT)

God Always Has a **Plan B**

for Helping Us Do Love's Hard Work

What is love? Scan the radio Top 40 or the TV listings, and the word pops up like dandelions.

Unfortunately, the love portrayed in modern media often isn't the real deal. The "love" many singers profess, for example, is selfish obsession, lacking depth. Or it's a whim, usually driven by physical attraction. "I love you, Baby!" in a pop song is better translated, "I am hot for you at this present moment—until someone more attractive than you comes into the picture."

God, the author of love, didn't design it to be a mere feeling. Yes, love is emotional. But it is also a decision, an act of will. Sometimes, love is struggle, something that requires constant effort. True love is caring about another person—your spouse, kids, parents, and (gulp) parents-in-law—even if your love isn't reciprocated or even appreciated. Love is a commitment that doesn't fade, regardless of consequences.

Real love is what Jesus displayed for the world when He chose to sacrifice Himself for all of us. And He made this choice *knowing* that many would spurn or belittle His supreme sacrifice. Further, He knew that no one deserved this great gift of love. He knows the selfishness of the human heart. He knows every awful thing about every single person who has ever lived—or ever will live. Yet, He still gave Himself up.

The Lord of all creation, who knew you before you were born, has decided to love you—in spite of mistakes. In spite of the indifference you might feel toward Him sometimes. God loves you. He is committed to you. He will faithfully forgive, unconditionally accept, and perfectly love you always. He makes the effort, every day. And He wants us to try to do the same.

Whoever does not love does not know God, because God is love.

1 John 4:8

for Giving You the Time of Your Life

"Time will take your money, but money won't buy time."

James Taylor

Imagine this: Tomorrow morning you wake up and check your savings account balance, and you discover that someone has deposited $86,400 in your account. You are sure it's some kind of computer error—until the following day, when the same thing happens. And the day after that, too.

Nice fantasy, huh? Well, the truth is that you do have an account like this—sort of. You could label this account Time. Every morning, you get a fresh 86,400 seconds credited to you. The catch, of course, is that yesterday's seconds do not accrue. The time you fail to use wisely is lost. With time, there are no carryovers, no overdrafts.

Some people say, "Time is money," but there are big differences between the two. You can't hoard time. You can't store it or borrow against it. You can't lend your time to someone else.

With time, you use it or you lose it.

As you think about how to use your daily allotment of 86,400 seconds, keep these principles in mind:

1. You can't really manage time, despite what the efficiency experts say. But you can manage the things, people, and processes that take up your time.

2. Time is expensive. Business expert Lewis Timberlake estimates that 80 percent of the average businessperson's day is spent on things or people that yield only 2 percent of his or her results.

3. Time (as we have already noted) is perishable. It can't be saved for later use.

4. Time is a great equalizer. Everybody gets that same amount of daily seconds: popes, paupers, presidents, princesses, and pop stars alike. Success isn't about how much time one possesses; it's all about how much time one uses.

5. Time is irreplaceable. "Making up for lost time" is a misnomer. When time has passed, it is gone.

6. Time is ruled by priorities. You have enough time for just about anything—as long as that anything ranks high enough on your priority list. Keep careful track of your days and note if low-priority busywork or interruptions are robbing you of time from what is really important to you.

How many times do you hear someone say, "Oh, if only I had more time!"? How many times is that "someone" you? Don't be deceived. The president of the United States has no more time than you do. The vagrants on the street have no less. God gives every woman and man a possibility-rich twenty-four hours every day. How you spend those 86,400 seconds reveals what really makes you tick.

So manage your time. Don't let it manage you.

Make the most of every opportunity in these evil days.

Ephesians 5:16 (NLT)

God Always Has a **Plan B**

for Taking You Places (All Kinds of Places)

"All journeys that really matter start deep inside of us."

Michelle Perry

Michelle Perry was born without a left kidney, hip, or leg. By the time she was thirteen years old, she had had endured twenty-three operations. Despite her physical challenges, Michelle was a mover. She got around just fine on one leg and crutches. She navigated quickly and confidently in other respects as well. Before her seventeenth birthday, she was a sought-after motivational speaker, a leadership trainer, and a published writer. At seventeen, she began college at Baylor University in Waco, Texas.

One Sunday morning, Michelle heard singing from her Baylor dorm room. She wandered outside to investigate. Eventually she found the source of the singing: an open-air worship service being held under a bridge along Interstate 35. Called, appropriately, the Church Under the Bridge, this particular congregation was composed of bikers, prostitutes, alcoholics, the homeless, and other assorted street people.

Not one to be intimidated, Michelle stayed for the rest of the service, finding a flimsy folding chair between one man who reeked of alcohol and another who just plain *reeked*. She sat and took in the whole experience: The children laughing as they took part in the Sunday school nearby. The congregants who took turns pouring out their hearts, and the cars whooshing by on the overpass. She was struck by one thought: "I bet Jesus would like it here. He would feel right at home."

Soon, Michelle began volunteering at the Church Under the Bridge. As the weeks rolled by, she sensed that God's love might be best experienced in unconventional places like this. Michelle's duties included teaching the church's children. She quickly learned that no traditional Bible curriculum was going to work with the kids of bikers, prostitutes, and the like. The only way to reach these kids was to love them.

She prayed fervently for the ability to show Jesus' love. As she talked with the kids and answered their questions about her physical challenges, she strived to embody love in all she did and said.

Eventually, Michelle left Baylor and her open-air church to spend a few years ministering in Calcutta, India. She returned to the United States, securing a job as a graphic designer serving several ministries in Colorado Springs, Colorado. Compared to what she had experienced as a teenager and young twenty-something, her life was comfortable— perhaps too comfortable. She knew something was missing.

Sitting at her kitchen table one day in 2005, she turned on her TV. While channel surfing, she stumbled on a show about the children of Darfur, a region of Sudan. She was intrigued by the sight of a white Western woman in the midst of a multitude of dark African children, their skin tinged red from the dust they sat in. The children were showing the woman crayon pictures of Kalashnikov rifles and of their families being torn apart by war. One little boy showed a picture of his family running in different directions as "birds" rained down fire from above.

As she watched, Michelle felt hot tears sliding down her cheeks. She was flooded with compassion for those children. She knew it was time to move on from Colorado.

Thirteen months later, Michelle found herself working in the southern Sudanese village of Yei, serving as the founding field coordinator for a mission called Iris Ministries. In one sense, she was far from home, but she had come to believe that home was no longer a specific geographic place, it was wherever God wanted her to be.

Michelle found Sudan to be a place of unimaginable challenges, overwhelming heartbreaks, and faith-affirming miracles, all at the same time. When she traveled in the area, children would run alongside her car, shouting, "Kwaja, jibu guruush." ("White person, give me money.") Roads were patrolled by men with AK-47 assault rifles in one hand and bottles of booze in the other.

The mission opened with a celebration feast on Christmas Day 2006. Michelle believed the feast would draw at least a thousand people. She made the bone-jarring drive from Yei to Uganda to buy supplies, including a cow. Upon returning she discovered that the contractors she had hired to refurbish Iris Ministries' main building had left with her money without doing any of the work. Meanwhile, the cow (who was to be a source of milk) somehow disappeared.

But Michelle insisted that the feast would go on. She searched and searched and finally found the wayward cow. Then she blanketed the surrounding area with invitations to the banquet.

On the big day, only a few people showed up, even with the promise of free food. So Michelle sent volunteers into the streets. They invited anyone and everyone. Soon, United Nations officials and local government big shots were dining with peasants dressed in rags. More than a thousand people were fed, and, more importantly, Michelle found twelve orphans who would live, learn, and grow at Iris Ministries.

Anyone even remotely familiar with life in the Sudan knows that it is a constant test of faith, conviction, and mettle. Though many consider southern Sudan "Christian," even most of the region's professing Christians still hold deep superstitions about the power of spirits and witchcraft. Michelle finds herself quoting Ephesians 6:12 (ESV) almost every day: *"For we do not wrestle against flesh and blood, but against the rulers, against the authorities, against the cosmic powers over this present darkness, against the spiritual forces of evil in the heavenly places."*

Michelle often wakes in the middle of the night, shaken from sleep by the sounds of gunfire. Walking Iris' perimeter in the morning, she sometimes finds new bullet holes in the sides of various buildings.

New people show up on her doorstep almost every day. Some bring orphaned children. Others beg for money. A few try to swindle her. And then there are the sick and the injured, looking for medical treatment.

Despite the constant challenges, Michelle is regularly amazed at how often simple prayers of faith are answered, and how the joy on one child's face can wipe away an entire day of dust, setbacks, and disappointments. She believes in a God who can handle the impossible.

Why does Michelle Perry choose to live this life? Because, for her, southern Sudan is the land of God's heart. During its first two years, Iris Ministries took in eighty children, hired a staff of twenty full-time workers, started a school, developed training seminars, and planted a handful of churches.

When asked about her "strategic plan" for accomplishing so much, Michelle has a ready answer:

Step One: Every morning, wake up.

Step Two: Ask Jesus what He is doing that day—not what He *wants* you to do, but what He is already doing.

Step Three: Go join Him.

Michelle has come to realize that for love to have a face to people who don't know God, someone has to offer *her* face. As a result, people in and around the village of Yei are seeing Jesus in one brave woman's eyes every day.

Michelle (or Mama, as she is known in Yei) knows she is making a difference when she hears words like these from a Sudanese man:

"We have seen religion, but this is love. That is why, Mama, you are so different. No one has ever seen this here before. I am an old man. We have seen aid, we have seen religion, and we have seen programs. But we have never seen love. Until now. That is why you have come."

If you spend yourselves in behalf of the hungry and satisfy the needs of the oppressed, then your light will rise in the darkness, and your night will become like the noonday.
Isaiah 58:10

God Always Has a **Plan B**

for Teamwork That Makes Dreams Work

*"For a community to be whole and healthy, it must be based
on people's love and concern for each other."*

Millard Fuller

"This is my domain, my turf!" For many women, "my turf" means the
kitchen, the pantry, or even the wine cellar. And we don't like that turf
to be invaded.

Indeed, when someone messes with our food or beverages, even the
calmest among us can freak out.

So you can imagine the horror endured by the owners of a meat-
packing plant when they discovered that someone—or some *thing*—
was eating huge hunks of meat that were hanging on high hooks
to age. Every morning, workers would enter the plant and find that
chunks of meat had been knocked to the floor and devoured.

Desperate, they hired an exterminator to hide in the plant overnight
to catch the meat thief.

That exterminator was amazed by what he saw when night fell: A
swarm of rats snuck into the building. Then, one by one, they formed
a tall rat pyramid. Next, one rat scrambled its way up the pyramid and
leaped onto a hunk of beef. He then chewed the meat around the hook

until the whole thing crashed to the floor. At that point, hundreds of rats pounced on their dinner and ate themselves silly.

As unappetizing as it might be, let's think about those clever rats for a bit. The rats at the bottom of the pyramid had to be strong and hold very still. The rats near the top had to be nimble as they climbed up, over, and around their rodent teammates. And, even though they were oh-so-close to the meat, they had to keep their place so that one of their rat buddies could accomplish the final task of crashing dinner to the floor.

The lesson here: Asking for help isn't a sign of weakness and neither is being part of a team or a group. Sometimes it is the smart thing to do, even for the most independent-minded woman. The Bible tells us that two people working together can accomplish more than one person trying to go it alone. So don't be afraid to ask for help. And keep in mind that the person *you* seek help from today just might be the person who needs your help tomorrow!

Two people are better off than one, for they can help each other succeed. If one person falls, the other can reach out and help. But someone who falls alone is in real trouble.

Ecclesiastes 4:9-10 (NLT)

God Always Has a **Plan B**

for Proving That Age Is Just a Number

"The real trick is to stay alive as long as you live."

Ann Landers

"Old age is always fifteen years older than I am," goes the famous adage. Whatever "old" is to you, it's a place you're in no hurry to reach. Women and men alike fear how age will affect them—mentally and physically. They can't imagine being as happy as they are now when they're "old."

Surprisingly, though, older people are just as happy as younger people. Many senior citizens report a serene sense of satisfaction with life. Further, what is possible at various ages is continually being redefined.

Consider...

• Swimmer Dara Torres won three Olympic silver medals at age forty-one (while competing in her fifth Olympic Games). At forty-five, she barely missed qualifying for her sixth Olympics—by just nine one-hundredths of a second.

• Actress Susan Sarandon didn't receive the first of her three Academy Awards until age forty-five, and now in her mid-sixties, she is still a leading lady on the silver screen.

- Comic actress Betty White hosted TV's *Saturday Night Live* for the first time at age eighty-eight after a campaign by her thousands of devoted fans. Now in her early nineties, she continues to appear in TV shows, specials, and commercials.

- At the age of fifty-three, Geraldine Wesolowski actually gave birth to her own grandson. She was implanted with an egg from her daughter-in-law and fertilized by her son. She carried the baby to term as a literal labor of love.

- And (as you can read elsewhere in this book) Grandma Moses didn't even *begin* her marvelous painting career until she was seventy-eight.

Today, advances in nutrition and medicine keep doors of opportunity open wider and longer than ever before. Couple these advances with the experience and wisdom that come with age, and you have a formula for success and happiness that defies "old" stereotypes.

Stories like the ones above (and a variety of studies and surveys) point to one ageless fact: Age is simply unrelated to one's level of personal happiness. Whatever your age, this year can be the happiest and most successful of your life.

Surely your goodness and love
will follow me all the days of my life.

Psalm 23:6

God Always Has a **Plan B**

for Creating Everyday Heroes

*"People see God every day;
they just don't recognize him."*

Pearl Bailey

A few years ago, a paralyzed veteran wrote the following letter to his then-unborn baby boy:

Son,

Your mother is very special. Few men know what it's like to receive appreciation for taking their wives out to dinner—when it entails what it does for us. It means she has to dress me, shave me, brush my teeth, comb my hair, wheel me out of the house and down the steps, open the garage, put me in the car, go around to the other side of the car, start it up, back it out, get out of the car, close the garage, get back in the car, and drive to the restaurant.

Then it starts all over again. She gets out of the car, unfolds the wheelchair, opens the door, spins me around, stands me up, seats me in the wheelchair, pushes the pedals out, closes the door and locks the car, wheels me into the restaurant, then takes the pedals off the wheelchair so I won't be uncomfortable. We sit down to have dinner, and she feeds me throughout the entire meal.

When it's over, she pays the bill, pushes the wheelchair out to the car again, and reverses the same routine. When it's all over, she says with true warmth, "Honey, thank you for taking me out to dinner."

I never quite know what to say in response. This *is the woman who is your mother.*

– Dad

As this letter proves (so poignantly), common, everyday tasks become heroic when they are done with love. Let us strive to go about our daily routines with the same dedication and care displayed by this wife, mom, and hero!

Serve one another in love.

Galatians 5:13 (NLT)

God Always Has a **Plan B**

for Helping "the Least of These"

"Every day we are called to do small things with great love."

Mother Teresa

Agnes was like many other Albanian girls born in the early 1900s. She loved her mother and father. She loved singing in her church choir.

But tragedy invaded Agnes's life early. Her father died when she was only eight. But instead of making Agnes and her mother bitter or depressed, the tragedy made them more compassionate. They regularly invited complete strangers to eat with them in their home.

When she was twelve, Agnes felt a sense of divine calling. She believed that God wanted her to dedicate her life to helping people affected by tragedy, hunger, and disease.

Agnes became a nun at age eighteen and began teaching at a convent school, where she was known as Sister Mary Teresa. She found teaching to be extremely rewarding, but at the same time, she felt that her childhood calling had not been completely fulfilled.

At age thirty-six, Mary Teresa decided to give her life to the poor. She moved to the slums of Calcutta, India, to minister to, in her words, "the unwanted, the unloved, the uncared for."

In the years that followed, Sister Mary Teresa did just that. She founded a leper colony, a nursing home, a family clinic, and launched a network of mobile health clinics to serve those who could not travel to get medical assistance and health resources.

As time went by, Sister Mary Teresa became Mother Teresa. She became famous for caring for the poor, the sick, and the needy. This was her life's work until the day she died at age eighty-seven.

Certainly, Mother Teresa is one of the most admired women in history. However, in recent years, new information has come to light—information that shows that though Mother Teresa might be a saint, she was also just like us in many ways. In her private correspondence, she shared time and again her doubts about her faith, her dark nights of the soul. Moreover, she expressed frustration and sadness over the monumental size of her task. At times, it seemed the needy far outnumbered those willing or able to meet those needs. Thus, she sometimes wondered if she was really making a difference.

But Mother Teresa kept on serving. Perhaps what is most admirable about her is that she did not let doubt and discouragement paralyze her. And even though her mind was sometimes troubled, her heart remained in the right place.

"As to my heart," she said near the end of her life, "I belong entirely to the Heart of Jesus."

May we all live and serve with that kind of heart.

If you help the poor,
you are lending to the Lord—
and he will repay you!

Proverbs 19:17 (NLT)

If you have enjoyed this book
or it has touched your life in some way,
we would love to hear from you.

Please send your comments to:
Hallmark Book Feedback
P.O. Box 419034
Mail Drop 215
Kansas City, MO 64141

Or e-mail us at:
booknotes@hallmark.com

KANSAS

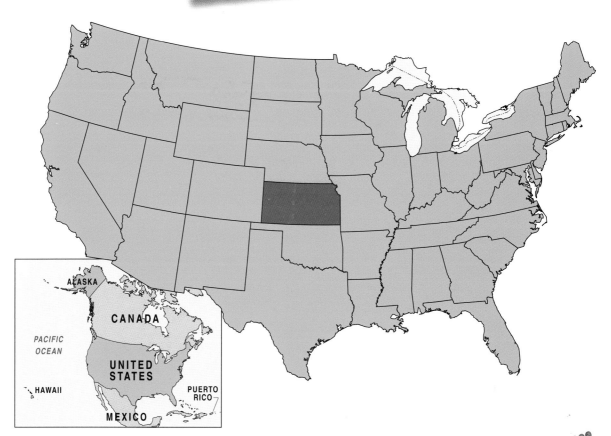

ALASKA

CANADA

PACIFIC
OCEAN

UNITED
STATES

HAWAII

PUERTO
RICO

MEXICO